ALEXANDER RODCHENKO

Alexander Rodchenko

Introduction by Serge Lemoine

PANTHEON BOOKS, NEW YORK

CENTRE NATIONAL DE LA PHOTOGRAPHIE, PARIS

Cover: Young woman with Leica, 1934.

Library of Congress Cataloging-in-Publication Data

Rodchenko, Aleksandr Mikhaïlovich, 1891–1956.
Alexander Rodchenko.

(Pantheon photo library)

Translated of: Alexsandre Rodtchenko. Paris:
Centre national de la photographie, © 1986.

1. Photography, Artistic. 2. Rodchenko, Aleksandr Mikhaïlovich,
1891–1956. I. Centre National de la Photographie (France) II. Title.
III. Series.
TR653.R6313 1987   779'.92'4   87-42620
ISBN 0-394-75424-X

Manufactured in Italy

691120

FROM THE EASEL TO THE MACHINE

Alexander Rodchenko (1891-1956) was a painter and a sculptor, a typographer, a poster artist, a furniture designer, a set decorator, an interior architect, and a teacher. And not least, he was a photographer, one of the most famous of the 20th century. During the 1920s he was one of the first artists, along with Moholy-Nagy, to become interested in photography. He discovered its technical virtues and its power to evoke. It enabled him to expound the highly personal vision so crucial to his work as an artist. A quick review of his career will help clarify this.

In the Soviet Union Rodchenko was the true leader of the artistic movement known as Constructivism. This was a style of art that sought to place emphasis on the materials used and to show how form can be derived from construction. In Constructivism, dynamic structures were employed in a novel space, and the focus was on the logic of the expression and the mastery of technique. To attain these objectives, Rodchenko was inspired by existing methods and forms, particularly in the scientific world, and even more so in the technical and industrial world. Constructivism defined itself as being a "materialist," mechanical – machine-like – art, in direct contact with reality and life. In *Art Isms* (1925) Lissitzky and Arp defined it as follows: "These artists see the world solely through the prism of technique... Constructivism proves that between mathematics and art, between an object of art and a technical invention, the line cannot be drawn."[1]

Within this movement, Rodchenko's career was exemplary. Beginning in 1915, he executed his first nonfigurative works, using a ruler and compass and only black and white paint to create contrasts in shapes. At this time he met Vladimir Tatlin, whose counter-reliefs would influence him profoundly. He was also influenced by Kazimir Malevich, even in his later collages of 1918-19, and for some time

1. Lissitzky and Arp, *Die Kunstismen*, Zurich, 1925 (republished in facsimile, New York, 1968).

he continued to define himself in relation to the creator of Suprematism. His painting *Black on Black* (1918) was his response to Malevich's *White Square on a Black Background.* He had not quite abolished forms entirely, because in this painting two superimposed half-moons and a circle can be distinguished. Rodchenko went even further in his "absolute" extremism (Marcel Duchamp had already experimented with this in another vein), which consisted of wanting to paint "the ultimate painting," as Nikolai Tarabukin put it,[2] i.e. the purest and most absolute work. At the "$5 \times 5 = 25$" exhibition in Moscow in 1921, Rodchenko's most notable contribution was a triptych composed of three canvases of the same size, each a monochrome – one red, one yellow, and one blue *(Pure Colors: Red, Yellow, Blue).* This triptych was considered "pure" painting, the be-all and end-all of painting. It was also the first entirely monochromatic painting, generating a series of experiments and research that pervaded 20th-century painting up until the time of Yves Klein.

Moreover, Rodchenko stressed "the primacy of the line: the single element that makes it possible to construct and create."[3] In his paintings, therefore, the accent is on dynamic structure, realized through the use of intersecting obliques, and on construction, as illustrated in *Construction avec lignes,* with its neutral background and anonymous facture. The line allows him to exclude form, color, composition, and technique. No doubt this "linearism" enabled him to move easily into the execution of spatial structures.

Three years after his first and still highly Suprematist experiments in sculpture in 1918, he transposed the context of his research on the line to space. He created works that were suspended from a wire, thus appearing to deny their mass and, with no pedestal, to negate gravity. He began to investigate modular systems and, despite a vocabulary and materials reduced to their most basic expression, achieved a wide variety of compositions.

Following a logical sequence in his work, he and his wife Varvara Stepanova (1884-1958) turned their attention to applied art. They made "products" of general usefulness – in this instance, posters for publicity, business and propaganda. They worked most frequently with the writer Vladimir Mayakovsky, who wrote the texts and slogans for the posters and became a close friend. Rodchenko also did magazine covers, layouts, and illustrations for printed works; for these, he liked to use the photomontage method. He also worked on films and in the theater, notably with Meyerhold. A more direct demonstration of his involvement in "real life" was his designing work clothes. In 1925 he travelled to Paris for the international exhibition of decorative arts. He was in charge of decorating the Soviet pavilion, built by Konstantin Melnikov. His design and execution at this show of a fully furnished and accessorized interior for a "workers' club" was widely acclaimed.

Rodchenko was, to state the obvious, an experimenter. Whatever draws one's interest to him, the thing that is most striking is the variety of methods he employed. Photography was not the least among them. After years of using other people's photographs in the collages and photomontages that he made for posters (e.g. the one for Dziga Vertov's *Kino-Glaz* in 1924) or to illustrate books (like the collection of poems by Mayakovsky *Pro Eto* [About This] in 1923), he decided to take up photography himself. Nothing is surprising in this decision. A Bolshevik and a Constructivist, Rodchenko belonged to the most radical artistic movement of the day: "Productivism." Other members were artists who exhibited anonymously with the association the Obmokhu[4] – the Stenberg brothers, Konstantin Medunetzky, Karel Ioganson, and the theoretician Alexei Gan, who declared "unconditional war on art." Painting and sculpture were to be considered only laboratory work, that is, research which was acceptable and tolerated only because it subsequently made it possible to produce utilitarian works.

This line quickly led to the overthrow of artistic endeavor and to the demand that only utilitarian works be produced and that "pure" art be abandoned. They pronounced "art and its high priests outlaws."[5] In 1921 Rodchenko and Stepanova published their *Manifesto of Productivism,* in which they proclaimed, "Down with art, long live technical science."[6] This was

2. Nikolai Tarabukin, *Le Dernier Tableau,* Paris, 1972. Texts chosen and introduced by Andrei B. Nakov.

3. Rodchenko's notes on "the line" were written in 1921 and were later published by Andrei B. Nakov in *Art Press,* no. 7, Paris, Nov.-Dec. 1973.

4. See Andrei B. Nakov, *Abstrait-Concret,* Paris, 1982.

5. As declared by the manifesto "Constructivists Address the World," published in 1921 by the Stenberg brothers and Medounetsky, quoted by Andrei B. Nakov in *2 Stenberg 2 la période "laboratoire" 1919-1921 du constructivisme russe,* Jean Chauvelin Gallery, Paris, Annely Juda Gallery, London, Art Gallery of Ontario, Toronto, 1975.

6. Quoted in the *Tendenzen der Zwanziger Jahre* exhibition catalogue, Berlin, 1977, p. 102.

the source of Rodchenko's recurring reference to the aesthetics of machinery and to the forms found within the industrial world, in factories, transformers, blast furnaces, dams, silos, airplanes, and ocean liners. The title of an essay published by Tarabukin in 1922 says it plainly: "From the Easel to the Machine."[7] In agreement with the Bolshevik doctrine of the time, Productivism proclaimed the social uselessness of works of art and demanded the creation of models for industrial production, the only criterion being that they serve a utilitarian purpose. Under such conditions the artist became an engineer working within the context of industry to create new technologies and turn out products necessary for society.

Ultimately, with principles based on such criteria as social usefulness and economic profitability, Productivism could be seen as leading to the demise of art and the disappearance of the artist. This is why in 1924 Rodchenko saw the numerous advantages that photography offered, particularly in the light of the changes in the Bolshevik regime's attitude since before Lenin's death concerning avant-garde art, changes that eventually led to its condemnation and ultimately to its total and definitive eradication.[8]

Photography was a new, modern technique. It turned out a product – the picture – by using a machine – the camera. Taking the picture, developing it, printing it were all mechanical, calculated operations. The equipment – camera, enlarger, film, paper, chemicals – was all industrially made. And, more important in view of Rodchenko's particularly "abstract" tendencies, photography let him once again create images of reality. The subject was thus reintroduced, without the artist having to paint it or manufacture it himself. Portraits and figures, cityscapes, architecture, pictures of industrial and agricultural activities, reports on the army, sports and life in a circus – all were images that were meant to be published. They were used as illustrations in magazines and books or were shown in propaganda exhibitions. They were presented without touch-ups, arranged according to the page layout required by the publication, *The USSR in Construction,* for example. They provided the material for photomontages that would be used as magazine covers *(Novyi Lef),* book jackets (Mayakovsky's *To Serge Essenin)* or posters *(Knigi).*

Whether they were posed because of technical difficulties arising from the shot or the requirements of framing, whether they were snapshots taken for a news report, or whether they were cropped and reframed during development or more rarely left in "full frame," all these photos demonstrate Rodchenko's assertive style.

Take, for example, the 1934 photo *Young Girl with a Leica*.[9] One is immediately struck by the composition. Rodchenko still saw the image as a rectangular surface defined by its four angles and structured by the diagonals that traverse it (the bench in relation to the figure), where the emphasis is on dissymmetry (the person is seated in the upper corner). Thanks to this use of counterpoint, bringing into play the respective weight of the represented plastic elements, Rodchenko manages a "balanced unbalance" according to the laws of Constructivism: construction through lines, construction through mass, and construction through light. The artist uses contrast between light elements and dark areas. Here, a particular effect is added: the shadow of a balustrade distributes the black and white elements in the composition, again according to the principles of dissymmetry.

To add to the tilt of the image he more often than not chose an exaggerated perspective angle, using either the extreme high or low angle shot, as for the scenic view of *The Canal to the White Sea* (1933) or the portrait *Pioneer with Trumpet* (1930). Applying the principle that lets the photographer pull up or completely tilt the horizon line neutralizes the depth of field and flattens the image. Rodchenko's photographic research testifies to the originality and power of his vision as well as his capacity to transfigure the represented reality. But it must also be stressed that with this particular means of expression he had found the exact equivalent of his constructivist paintings and sculptures without ever giving the impression that he employed or ever had recourse to artificial devices.

Photography held an important place in Rodchenko's career, which was marked both by the evolution of his own ideas and by the changing Soviet policies regarding the avant-garde artists, who encouraged a certain form of photographic and cinematographic activity for the purposes of propaganda. The logical result of his Productivist commitment was that he cease all artistic activity; after 1921, no paintings or sculpture by Rodchenko can be found, for it would

7. Tarabukin, *Le Dernier Tableau*.

8. Malevich, it must be remembered, was imprisoned twice under this regime.

9. This refers to the camera used to take the picture, and not to the model.

have been impossible, even had he wanted to, to return to his previous experiments.[10] Rodchenko devoted himself more and more exclusively to photography, until it became the only means by which he could express himself.

This would only be for a limited amount of time, however. Beginning in 1928 he was obliged to justify himself against charges of producing "propaganda of a nature foreign to the proletariat."[11] In 1931 he was reproached for "steering proletarian art toward Western advertising, formalism, and aesthetics."[12] Gradually he lost commissions and contacts, and no photographs are dated after 1941. A firm Communist, Rodchenko was in turn a victim of the system that he had helped bring into being and which revealed itself as one of the most gigantic misery-producing systems in history.

Alexander Rodchenko exerted great influence in the field of photography, particularly in the Soviet Union. This was all the more true in that he had no real competition. Soviet photography, subjected to the need to illustrate economic and social activity, never really rose above the mediocre, despite the real talent of photographers like Max Alpert or Arcadi Chaiket. Nothing was produced – in the rather similar conditions of the two social contexts – that can compare with the human depth, the artistic form, and the poetic quality of the American photographers of the Farm Security Administration: Dorothea Lange, Ben Shahn (also a painter), Walker Evans, Russell Lee, and Arthur Rothstein.

The members of the October Group, which he rejoined in 1928 – photographers such as Boris Ignatovich, Jakob Halib, Gueorgui Petroussov – had been marked by Rodchenko's aesthetics and subject matter. Other photographers elsewhere were also marked by these very elements, for example, the Productivist artists Mieczyslaw Szczuka and Mieczyslaw Berman in Poland. That Rodchenko was accorded no more appreciation as a photographer in his country than any other photographer was demonstrated in the official selection of the USSR at the *Film und Foto* exhibition at the Deutscher Werkbund in Stuttgart in 1929, for which Lissitzky designed the Soviet pavilion.[13] Yet he had had a profound effect on the photographic world in the Soviet Union. It went beyond the avant-garde and photographic circles, as demonstrated by the picture magazines from the forties and fifties – magazines like *The USSR in Construction*. In the area of the photographic image (as in typography, poster design, and advertising),

Rodchenko's art greatly contributed to forging the aesthetics of socialist realism.

Alexander Rodchenko, however, was not alone in this. He has now found his place on the international level,[14] but in his day he went unnoticed in other countries. He is missing, for instance, from the book by Franz Roh and Jan Tschichold, *Foto Auge,* published in 1929, whose cover is a photomontage by Lissitzky. Above all, there was Laszlo Moholy-Nagy, whose work can be compared with his: Moholy-Nagy's 1934 *Portrait of Oskar Schlemmer* and Rodchenko's *Young Girl with a Leica* have more than a few points in common – they are exactly alike. But Moholy-Nagy, often a step ahead, proved perhaps to be more inventive, more ambitious and more brilliant. In the final analysis it is those very same self-imposed and regime-inflicted ideological constraints that make Rodchenko's photographic work incomparable. *The Young Pioneer* and the *Head of a Young Girl* (1930) have become, through their framing and their meaning, unforgettable images, militant photos, and Constructivist works all testifying to a brutality and a force of conviction that may actually be preferable to the elegance of Moholy-Nagy. Through these works, Rodchenko succeeded, along with several other creators of the "new photography," in inventing brand new images, that is, new ways of seeing and showing the world. For the first time, the photo was not derived from models of painting: photography had become an art in itself.

Serge Lemoine

Translated by Marianne Tinnell Faure

10. Some paintings from the thirties are known, which are similar to what one can find in Paris at the Place du Tertre near Montmartre.

11. Quoted from the book by German Karginov, *Rodtchenko* (Paris, 1977), p. 227. He replied to it in an article "Mise en garde," published in *Novyi Lef,* no. 11, 1928, quoted in the catalogue *Rodtchenko Photographe,* Musée d'Art moderne de la Ville de Paris, Arc 2, 1977, prepared by Andrei B. Nakov.

12. Ibid.

13. In the catalogue from the *Film und Foto* exhibition, where Soviet participation was twice mentioned, twenty-two participants as well as an anonymous section are listed. Also among the works displayed were photos by Eisenstein, Kauffmann, Pudovkin, Vertov, Schub, plus film posters by Stenberg and Lissitzky, and photomontages by Klucis and Lissitzky. Rodchenko was represented by five works, including a portrait and two photos taken from illustrations that he had done for the children's book by Tretiako, *Samozveri.*

14. Western fascination with his work is in fact rather recent - since the end of the seventies. The book by Hubertus Gassner, *Rodcenko Fotografien* (Munich, 1982), provides excellent proof of this.

Linear construction, 1919.
(Geneva, Art and History museum).

1. Ossip Brik, 1924.

2. Vladimir Mayakovsky, 1924.

4. Vladimir Mayakovsky, 1924.

5. Vladimir Mayakovsky, 1924.

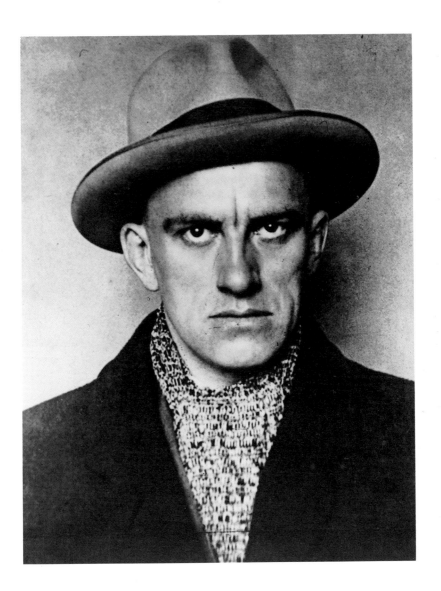

6. The artist's mother, 1924.

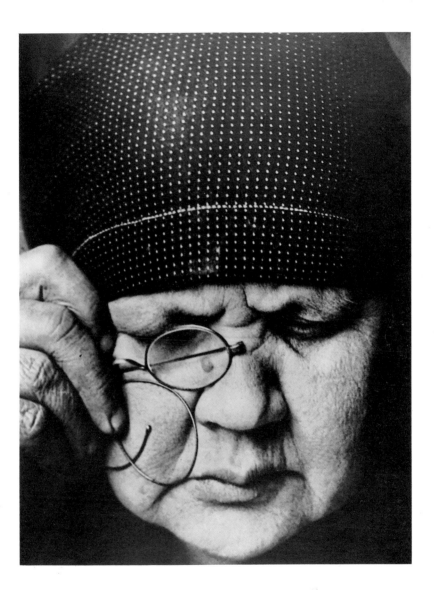

7. The balconies, 1925.

8. House in Miasnitzkaya Street, 1925.

9. Fire-escape ladder, 1925.

10. House in Miasnitzkaya Street, 1925.

11. Demonstration, 1920s.

12. Sergei Tretiakov, 1927.

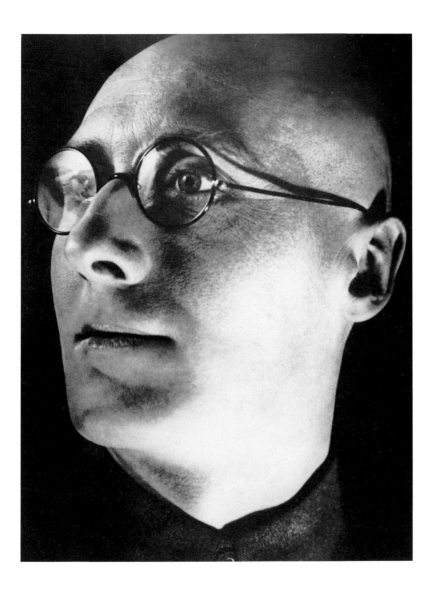

13. Esther Choub, film producer, 1924.

14. Courtyard, 1927.

15. Courtyard, 1927.

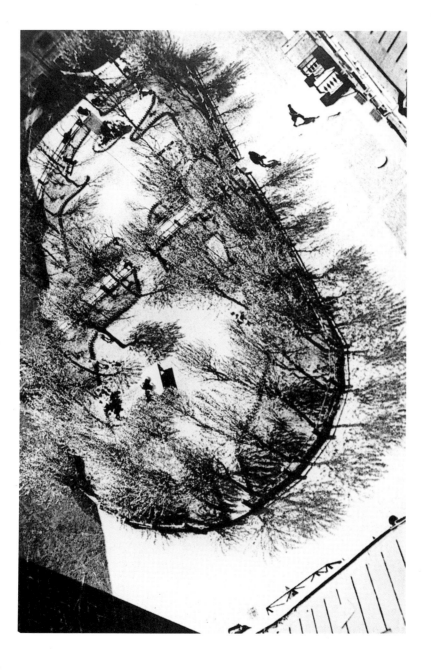

16. Courtyard, 1927.

17. Courtyard, 1927.

18. Student in a workers' school, 1927.

19. Brjansk Station, 1927.

20. Red Army soldier in a balloon, 1924.

21. On the telephone, 1928.

22. Miasnitzkaya Street (now Kirov Street), 1928.

23. Strastnaya Square, Moscow, 1928.

24. A street in Moscow, 1928.

25. The poet Nicolai Asseiev, 1927.

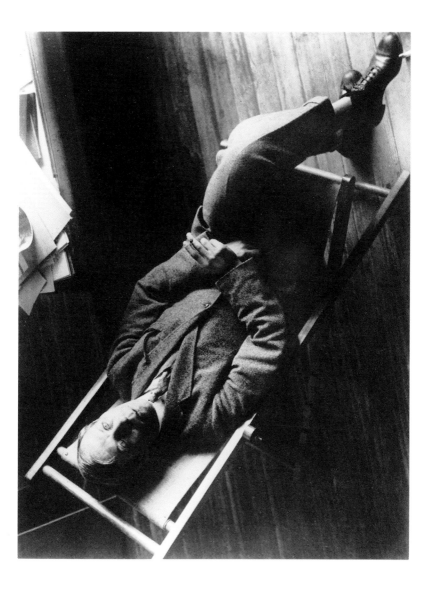

26. Pines, 1927.

27. Assembling before the demonstration, 1928.

28. Sawmill, 1928.

29. Printing plates, 1928.

30. Pioneer, 1928.

31. Orchestra, 1929.

32. Radio antenna, 1929.

33. The new Moguès, 1929.

34. Student, 1930.

35. Pioneer, 1930.

36. Pioneer, 1930.

37. The Bolshoi, 1930.

38. Staircase, 1930.

39. The White Sea Canal, 1933.

40. Sawmill: stacks of wood, 1931.

41. Park for culture and rest, a public holiday, 1931.

42. On the way to the demonstration, 1932.

43. Young woman with Leica, 1934.

44. Pioneer trumpet player, 1930.

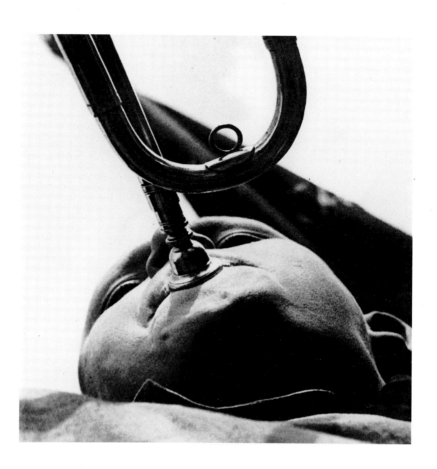

45. Chauffeur, 1933.

46. Gymnastics, 1932.

47. Circus, 1938.

48. Dive, 1936.

49. Dive, 1936.

GRAPHIC WORKS

50. Cover of the magazine *Novy Lef,* 1927.

новый
леф

№ 2
МОСКВА
1927

ЖУРНАЛ
левого фронта
искусств

ПОД РЕДАКЦИЕЙ

В. В. МАЯКОВСКОГО

ГОСИЗДАТ

51. Cover of the magazine *Novy Lef,* 1927.

№ 6

новый

леф

ГОСИЗДАТ

1927

52. Photomontage for Mayakovsky's *Pro Eto,* 1923.

Ловлю равновесие,
    страшно машу.

53. Photomontage for Mayakovsky's *Pro Eto*, 1923.

И она
— она зверей любила —
тоже ступит в сад.

54. Poster for Dziga Vertov's film *Kino Glaz* (Cinema Eye), 1924.

BLACK AND WHITE

The black Leica made of nickel and glass went happily
to work in his hands.

It would show him the world.
The world, quotidian and usual,
from a new angle.

More forcefully and more sublimely, it would show
men and the edification
of Socialism.
He would create propaganda with photography.
For all that is young, new and original.
But, then... the flight is cut short.
The red lamp is once again burning on the stage.
The room is black and deserted.
No flight...
No applause...
Criticism rains down on him full strength.
For his formalism, his foreshortenings
and all the rest.
He becomes once again a solitary child.
He is considered destructive and dangerous.
He is imitated, but spurned.
His friends are even afraid to go see him.
And so he decides to retire...
from the photographic scene, disappointed
and fatigued.

The homeland of Socialism no longer needs
ventriloquists, magicians, jugglers?
No fireworks, planetariums, flowers,
kaleidoscopes? ...
Fatigued, he is preparing for the Exhibition
of the Masters of Soviet Photographic Art.

He does not even know what to present.
No matter what, he would be criticized, and
will be criticized.
He thinks about it a long time. Is it worth
participating?
Finally, he makes up his mind.
And all of a sudden – success!
It had happened. Thundering applause.
He rises and begins to soar...
The infinite possibilities of creation
are once again open.
The room is filled with friends and acquaintances.
They want the flight.
They want the experiments and fantasy
of the little boy. All he ever dreamed about...

Rodchenko, taken from the artist's autobiography (1939) ; quoted in German Karginov, *Rodtchenko* (Paris, Editions du Chêne, 1977).

PHOTOGRAPHY-ART

It is difficult not to realize how hard we are trying to discover all the inherent possibilities of photography.

Like in a fairy tale or a wonderful dream, we are revealing the splendors of photography in their own staggering reality.

Applied photography, sometimes imitating copper engravings, sometimes painting, sometimes tapestries, found its path, is flourishing, and has left behind its own, strictly personal imprint. Unprecedented possibilities have opened up to it.

Images on several levels, such fineness that photomontage has been overtaken... Transitions ranging from the whole image to the finest lines.

Contradictions in perspective. Contrasts in light. Contrasts in forms. Views impossible to realize with drawing and painting. Foreshortenings grossly deforming objects, a harsh handling of matter.

Entirely new, never before seen moments in human, animal or machine movements.

Moments unknown to us, or which, if known, we cannot see, e.g. the trajectory of a bullet.

Compositions so audacious they surpass the imagination of painters, so rich in forms that Rubens has been left behind.

Compositions with such an extraordinarily complex interplay of lines that the Dutch and the Japanese cannot compare.

Then, there is the creation of instants which do not exist, that are produced on a photo, through montage.

The negative transmits entirely new stimuli to feelings.

I am not even talking of overlays, optical distortions, the fixing of reflections or other similar techniques.

Photographers have demonstrated that they are artists, with their own specific taste, style and manner. They work doggedly on their themes and styles.

Photography is advancing by giant steps and is conquering one field after another. It aspires to be as widespread as painting.

Technically, photography is simple and quick. It is so indispensable an accessory to science, life and technology that as such, as something easily attainable, it is not yet considered worthy of being its own prophet... It has been denied the right to have its very own creative artists, its own geniuses.

Love of photography must absolutely be encouraged to the point that people will start collecting photographs. Photo libraries must be established and big exhibitions organized. Instead of "salons," an international photographic exhibition should be organized. Books and magazines on photography should be published.

Photography has every right – and every reason – to be regarded as the art of our time.

Rodchenko, (1934), taken from German Karginov, *Rodtchenko* (Paris, Editions du Chêne, 1977).

BIOGRAPHY

1891. Born in St. Petersburg, November 23.

1910. Student at the School of Fine Arts in Kazan.

1914. Meets the Futurist poets Mayakovsky, Burliuk, and Kamensky at a public lecture in Kazan.

1915. Arrives in Moscow, where he attends the Stroganov School for a few months. Meets Tatlin.

1916. Meets Malevich and encounters the theory of Suprematism.

1917. Is named secretary of the Leftist Federation of Painters' Unions. Takes part in designing the interior of the Café Pittoresque, where art, literature, and theater would be presented.

1918. Holds an important position in the IZO Narkompros (Department of Visual Arts in the People's Commissariat for Enlightenment). Organizes the subsection of decorative arts with O. Rosanova. Takes active part in founding the Museum of Artistic Culture; acts as the museum's first director.

Late 1918-early 1919. Becomes interested in architecture and line structure; joins the Zhivskulptarkh - the painting/sculpture/architectural group.

1919. Does his first collages. Acts as president of the Federation of Painters of New Art.

1920. Member of the Inkhuk (Institute of Artistic Culture) in Moscow, established in May 1920. Professor at the Vkhutemas (technical studios of the higher state school of art). Becomes

a central figure in the productivist movement (design). Produces a series of unpublished collages for a book by Axionov, *The Pillars of Hercules.*

1921. At the "5 x 5 = 25" exhibition in September, shows three monochrome paintings: *Pure Colors: Red, Yellow, Blue.* These are the last easel paintings he produced.

1921-31. Works in theater and films.

1923. Takes active interest in advertising; colloborates closely with Mayakovsky. Does photomontages, notably eleven illustrations for Mayakovsky's poem *Pro Eto* (About This).

1923-28. Designs covers for *Lef* and *Novy Lef* magazines.

1924. Begins to take pictures for his photomontage work. Produces his first journalistic report, "Where They Make Money," a look at the workers and work process at the banknote printing office, Goznak, which is published in *Technology and Life* magazine.

1929. Has photos published in many magazines.

1930. Leaves teaching, after the Vkhutemas is closed. Joins the photography section of the October Group of artists.

1931. Membership in October Group revoked on charges of "propaganda of a nature foreign to the proletariat."

1931-32. Abandons reporting jobs for periodicals and does photographic sketches and series of photos published in albums and books on specific topics.

1933-41. Produces more than ten special issues for the magazine *SSSR na stroike* (USSR in Construction).

1935. Begins a series on the circus.

1935-40. Does a series of albums and books of photos with his wife, Varvara Stepanova.

1940. Contributes to the publication of a volume of selected works of Mayakovsky, who had died ten years earlier. Returns to abstract painting, in decorative style.

1941. Leaves Moscow with his family. Works in the Otchera section of the Molotov artists' alliance and for the newspaper *Starlinsky Udarnik*. Returns briefly to photography when he works with the newspaper *Stalinskaya Putovka*.

1942. Returns to Moscow in summer. Works in the Sovinform offices organizing exhibitions.

1944-45. Chief artistic advisor at Domtechnik.

1945-48. Produces anniversary albums with Varvara Stepanova: *25th Anniversary of the Republic of Kazakhstan, 30 Years of Soviet Literature.*

1949. Works with Varvara Stepanova on a series of posters on Mayakovsky. Begins stage sets for the Bolshoi's production of *Sleeping Beauty*, but falls ill.

1953. Works on a series of posters on agricultural themes.

1956. Works through the autumn with Varvara Stepanova on Mayakovsky's book *Pretty Good!* Dies on December 3.

BIBLIOGRAPHY

General works

1969. Gray, Camilla. **L'Avant-Garde russe dans l'art moderne.** Lausanne: Editions l'Age d'Homme.

1979. Film und Foto der zwanziger Jahre, exhibition catalogue, Württembergischer Kunstverein, Stuttgart.

1980. Werscher, Herta. **Die Geschichte der Collage, vom Kubismus bis zur Gegenwart.** Cologne: Du Mont Buchverlag.

1981. Von der Malerei zum Design, Russische Konstruktivistiche Kunst der zwanziger Jahre. Cologne: Galerie Gmurzynska.

1981. Van der Rudenstine, Angelica. **Russian Avant-Garde: The Georges Costakis Collection.** London: Thames and Hudson.

1981. Nakov, Andrei. **Abstrait/Concret: Art Non-figuratif Russe et Polonais.** Paris: Trans-edition.

1983. Chudakov, Gryori. **Pionniers de la Photographie russe soviétique.** Paris: Philippe Sers Editeur.

1984. Leclanche-Boulé, Claude. **Typographes et Photomontages constructivistes.** Paris: Editions Papyrus.

Books and Articles on Rodchenko

1965. Gray, Camilla. "A. Rodchenko: A Constructivist Designer," *Typographica,* no. 6.

1970. Boyko, S. "Collages et Photomontages oubliés de A. Rodchenko," *Opus International,* no. 3.

1977. Karginov, German. **Rodchenko.** Paris: Chêne.

Nakov, Andrei. **Rodtchenko photographe,** exhibition catalogue, Musée d'Art moderne de la Ville de Paris.

1978. Weiss, Evelyn. **Alexander Rodtschenko: Fotographien 1920-1938.** Wienand Verlag, 1978 – exhibition catalogue, Museum Ludwig, Cologne.

1979. Alexander Rodchenko, Exhibition catalogue, Museum of Modern Art, Oxford, 1979; reprint, New York: Pantheon Books (1980).

1981. Mayer, Rudolph. **Alexander Rodtschenko, Warwara Stepanova, Zeichnungen, Linolschnitte und Photographien.** Dresden: Staatliche Kunstsammlungen.

1982. Gassner, Hubertus, and Lavrentiev, Alexander. **Rodcenko Fotografien.** Munich: Schirmer/Mosel. **Alexandre Rodtchenko: Possibilités de la Photographie.** Cologne: Galerie Gmurzynska.

1983. Alexandre Rodtchenko. I Grandi Fotografi, serie argento. Milan: Gruppo Editoriale Fabbri. **Alexander Rodtschenko und Warwara Stepanova.** Exhibition catalogue, Wilhelm Lehmbruck Museum. Baden-Baden: Duisburg und Staatliche Kunsthalle.

1984. Gassner, Hubertus. **Alexander Rodtschenko Konstruktion 1920: Oder die Kunst, das Leben zur organisieren.** Frankfurt: Fisher Taschenbuch Verlag.

Writings by Rodchenko

1967. "O Vladimire Tatline, Années 1940" (On Vladimir Tatlin – the 1940s), *Opus International,* no. 4, Paris.

1971. "Fotografia-Iskousstvo, Tchernoie i Beloie" (Photography-Art, Black and White), *Sovietskoie Foto, Moscow.*

1973. "Moia Rabota s Maïakovskim" (My Work with Mayakovsky), 1939, *V Mire Knig,* no. 6, Moscow.

1974. "Liniia" (The Line), 1921, in *Von der Fläche zum Raum.* Exhibition catalogue, Galerie Gmurzynska, Cologne.

1975. "Remarks on Composition," 1920, in *Die Zwanziger Jahre in Osteuropa,* exhibition catalogue, Galerie Gmurzynska, Cologne.

1978. "Stati, Vospominania, Avtobiografitscheskie Zapiski, Pisma" (Articles, Reminiscences, Autobiographical Notes, Letters), Moscow.

EXHIBITIONS

1913. Second Temporary Exhibition at the School of Art, Kazan.

1916. "Magazine," a Futurist exhibition, Moscow.

1918. First Exhibition of the Federation of Artists, Moscow. "Five Years of Art," individual exhibition by Rodchenko at the Club of the Leftist Federation, Moscow.

1919. "Non-objective Creation and Suprematism," People's Commissariat of Public Enlightenment, Moscow.

1920. Exhibition in honor of the IIIrd Congress of the Communist Internationale, Moscow. "Zhivkulptura" (Painting-Sculpture), Moscow.

1921. "5 x 5 = 25," Moscow.

1922. First exhibition of Russian art, Berlin.

1923. "First Years of Theater Stage Settings in Moscow," Moscow.

1924. XIV Biennale, Venice.

1925. First exhibition of film posters, Moscow.
Exposition Internationale des Arts Décoratifs, Paris.

1926. Exhibition of Theater Art, National Institute of Cultural Relations, New York.

1928. "Ten Years of Soviet Photographic Art," Moscow and Leningrad.
VIIIth International Exhibition of Photographic Art, New York, Westminster.

1929. First International Season of Photographic Art, Chicago. First International Exhibition of Photographic Art, Vienna. « Film und Foto », Stuttgart and Berlin.

1930. Photographic exhibition of the October Group of artists, Moscow.

1931. Exposition Internationale de l'Art du Livre, Paris. "Fotomontage," Kunstgewerbemuseum, Berlin.

1933. "Fifteen Years of Art in the USSR," Moscow.

1937. XXXIIe Salon International de Photographie, Paris. Publications exhibited at the Soviet pavilion at the Universal Exhibition of Paris.

1939. VIe Salon International de Photographie, Charleroi.

1948. First Exhibition of Book Art, Moscow.

1955. Exhibition of Photographic Art, Moscow.

1957. First posthumous exhibition of Rodchenko's work, Journalists' Society, Moscow.

1961. Exhibition organized on the occasion of the 70th anniversary of Rodchenko's birth, Writers' Society, Moscow.

1962. "A. M. Rodchenko" (photographs, books, posters), Writers' Society, Leningrad.

1967. "East European Avant-Garde, 1910-1930," Berlin.

1968. "A. M. Rodchenko," Journalists' Society, Moscow.

1971. "The Art of Revolutionary Russia: Soviet Fine Arts and Decorative Art from 1917," London.
"A.M. Rodchenko," Museum of Modern Art, New York.

1974. "Von der Fläche zum Raum," Galerie Gmurzynska, Cologne.

1975. "Die zwanziger Jahre in Osteuropa," Galerie Gmurzynska, Cologne.

1977. "Rodtschenko Photographie," Musée d'Art moderne de la Ville de Paris.
"Photographs by 20th Century Artists," Hanover.

1978. "Photographs from the Sam Wagstaff Collection," Washington

"A. Rodtschenko Fotografien," Museum Ludwig, Cologne.

1979. "Alexander Rodchenko," Museum of Modern Art, Oxford. "Paris-Moscou, 1900-1930," Centre Georges Pompidou, Paris.

1980. "Utopies et Réalités en URSS 1917-1934," Centre Georges Pompidou, Paris.

1981. "Alexander Rodtschenko, Warwara Stepanova-Zeichnungen, Linolschnitte, und Photographien," Kupferstich-Kabinett, Dresden.

1982. "Photographie Soviétique 1917-1930," Musée des Arts Décoratifs, Paris.

1983. "Alexander Rodtschenko und Warwara Stepanova," Wilhem Lehmbruck Museum, Duisburg. Staatliche Kunsthalle, Baden-Baden.

PANTHEON PHOTO LIBRARY

American Photographers of the Depression
Eugène Atget
Henri Cartier-Bresson
Bruce Davidson
Early Color Photography
Robert Frank
André Kertész
Jacques-Henri Lartigue
Duane Michals
Helmut Newton
The Nude
Alexander Rodchenko
W. Eugene Smith
Weegee

The Pantheon Photo Library:
a collection conceived and produced by the
National Center of Photography in Paris
under the direction of Robert Delpire.